Contents

~ Welcome & What You'll Learn

Welcome & What You'll Learn

In today's rapidly evolving world, the ability to understand and harness the power of data has become a defining skill. From businesses and organizations to scientific research and government initiatives, data analytics plays a pivotal role in driving informed decisions, sparking innovation, and shaping the future.

If you're ready to embark on a journey of discovery and unlock the secrets hidden within data, then this book, "Data Analytics Decoded: A Beginner's Handbook," is your essential guide.

What This Book Is About

This book aims to break down the complexities of data analytics and make it accessible to everyone. Whether you're a student, a professional looking to switch career paths, or simply someone curious about the field, this handbook will provide you with a solid foundation. We'll cover:

- **Core concepts:** You'll gain a clear understanding of the fundamental principles, terminology, and frameworks that underpin the world of data analytics.
- **Data toolkit:** You'll explore various analytical tools, software, and techniques, learning how to choose the right ones for your needs.
- **The process of data analysis:** We'll walk you through the entire data analytics journey, from data collection and preparation to analysis, interpretation, and visualization.
- **Real-world applications:** You'll discover how data analytics is transforming industries, including healthcare, finance, marketing, and beyond.

How You'll Benefit

By the end of this book, you will have developed:

- **Data fluency:** You'll gain the confidence to speak the language of data and understand its significance in various contexts.
- **Problem-solving skills:** You'll be able to use data effectively to answer critical questions, address challenges, and make better decisions.
- **A competitive edge:** Your grasp of data analytics will make you a more valuable asset in any workplace or field.
- **An analytical mindset:** You'll learn to think critically, ask insightful questions, and see the world through a data-driven lens.

Get Ready to Dive In

Data analytics might seem a bit daunting at first, but we'll guide you every step of the way. We'll use clear language, real-life examples, and practical exercises to make the learning process both enjoyable and effective.

So, take a deep breath, get ready to expand your horizons, and let's dive into the fascinating world of data analytics together!

Additional Resources

- **Khan Academy: Introduction to Statistics**
  https://www.khanacademy.org/math/statistics-probability
- **DataCamp: Intro to Data for Data Science**
  https://www.datacamp.com/courses/introduction-to-data-for-data-science
- **Data Literacy Project: What is data literacy?**
  https://dataliteracy.com/

Section 1:
Introduction to the
World of Data

Data Unveiled: A Journey into Understanding

The Essence of Data

Data, in its simplest form, is a collection of raw facts, figures, observations, and measurements. It's everywhere, generated in massive quantities every second of every day. Think about your online activity: your search queries, social media likes, items in your shopping cart–it's all data. Every click, transaction, and sensor reading adds to the vast ocean of information that surrounds us.

But data itself is just a starting point. It's raw and often unstructured, offering little value in its original form. Think of it as a pile of puzzle pieces. The true magic of data lies in the insights it can hold when it's analyzed and interpreted effectively.

Why Data Matters

In today's world, data has become a currency, as valuable as gold or oil. Here's why data analytics matter:

- **Better decision-making:** Data-driven insights enable businesses, organizations, and individuals to make informed decisions based on evidence, rather than relying solely on gut feeling or intuition.

- **Identifying patterns and trends:** Data allows us to uncover hidden patterns and trends that might not be visible to the naked eye, leading to valuable predictions about customer behavior, market shifts, or emerging risks.
- **Problem-solving:** By analyzing data, we can pinpoint the root causes of inefficiencies, bottlenecks, or recurring issues, leading to targeted solutions.
- **Innovation and Optimization:** Data fuels innovation, helping businesses identify new opportunities, improve product design, and optimize processes.

Types of Data

Not all data is created equal. Understanding the different types of data will help you approach analysis in the right way:

- **Quantitative data:** Numerical data, representing quantities, counts, or measurements. Examples include sales figures, website traffic, and temperature readings.
- **Qualitative data:** Descriptive data, capturing characteristics, opinions, or perceptions. Examples include customer reviews, interview transcripts, and social media comments.
- **Structured data:** Data that can be easily organized into tables, databases, and spreadsheets, with well-defined rows and columns (e.g., transaction records).
- **Unstructured data:** Data that doesn't fit neatly into a predefined format, requiring more effort to organize and analyze (e.g., text documents, images, videos).

The Transformation of Data

Turning data into valuable insights is a multi-step journey, and this book will guide you through it. The journey often begins with a question or a problem you want to solve. Then follows:

1. **Data Collection:** Gathering data from relevant sources, such as surveys, experiments, log files, or third-party databases.
2. **Data Cleaning and Preparation:** Ensuring data quality by fixing errors, inconsistencies, and addressing missing values.
3. **Data Analysis:** Applying statistical techniques and analytical models to explore, visualize, and understand the data.
4. **Insights and Interpretation:** Turning analytical findings into actionable insights, communicating them effectively through reports or visualizations.

Let the Adventure Begin

Data analytics is an exciting field with the power to reshape industries, drive innovation, and ultimately improve our world. Get ready to see the world through a new lens as you uncover the stories hidden within data.

Additional Resources

- **Understanding the Different Types of Data**
  https://www.sisense.com/glossary/data-types/
- **The Data Journey explained in simple terms**
  https://www.cio.com/article/3491284/understanding-the-data-lifecycle.html

Unraveling the Data Puzzle: Exploring the Depths

In the previous chapter, we started to unveil the nature of data and its significance. Now, we'll dive deeper into the heart of what data can tell us, and how we can begin understanding its complexities.

Different Depths of Data

Think of data like an iceberg. What we see on the surface is only a small fraction of what lies beneath. Beneath the apparent numbers and facts are deeper layers of insights:

- **Descriptive:** This layer tells us the "what." It sums up past data to describe what has already happened. Examples: sales increased by 15%, website traffic peaked on Tuesday.
- **Diagnostic:** This layer answers the "why." It analyzes data to identify the factors or reasons behind certain trends, patterns, or events. Example: website traffic peaked due to a social media campaign.
- **Predictive:** This layer ventures into forecasting the "what if." Predictive analytics uses past data to build models that estimate the likelihood of future outcomes. Example: Based on past sales patterns, the model predicts a slow sales season.
- **Prescriptive:** This layer focuses on the "what should we do." It combines insights from previous levels with optimization techniques, recommending a course of action to achieve a desired outcome. Example: To boost sales, the model suggests increasing advertising in specific channels.

Data in Context

It's crucial to remember that data never exists in a vacuum. It always has a context—where it came from, how it was collected, what time period it represents. Context is critical to avoid misinterpretations.

To grasp context, ask yourself questions like:

- **Source:** Where did this data come from (e.g., an online survey, a sensor network, a sales database)?
- **Bias:** Are there any inherent biases in how the data was collected that could influence results?
- **Relevance:** How closely does the data relate to the specific question I'm trying to answer?
- **Timeliness:** Is this data an accurate reflection of the current situation or is it outdated?

Data Quality: Trust but Verify

Not all data is reliable. Errors, inconsistencies, and missing information can all undermine the insights you want to extract. Key aspects of data quality to keep in mind:

- **Accuracy:** Does the data correctly reflect real-world values?
- **Completeness:** Is all the necessary information present, or are there gaps?
- **Consistency:** Is the data formatted consistently throughout, allowing for easy comparisons?
- **Validity:** Does the data measure what you intend it to measure?

The Art of Asking Questions

Before you can analyze data effectively, you need to understand your goals. What specific questions do you want the data to answer? Asking the right questions will determine the direction of your analysis and which techniques will be most useful.

Example Questions

- "What are the key factors influencing our customer churn rate?"
- "Is there a seasonal pattern to our website traffic?"
- "Which marketing channels are generating the highest return on investment?"
- "Which products are frequently bought together?"

Let's Explore!

Unraveling the data puzzle is a thrilling adventure! In the following chapters, we'll learn about techniques to organize, visualize, and understand the data to uncover insights and tell compelling data stories.

Additional Resources

- **Data Storytelling: The Essential Data Science Skill Everyone Needs**
https://towardsdatascience.com/data-storytelling-the-essential-data-science-skill-everyone-needs-2b3c2fcf5baf
- **The 5 Critical Questions to Ask Before You Analyze Any Dataset**
https://towardsdatascience.com/the-5-critical-questions-to-ask-before-you-analyze-any-dataset-3d3eb7b6ef27

Navigating the Data Universe: A Comprehensive Overview

Embarking on Your Data Journey

The data universe is a realm of infinite possibilities for exploration. Before becoming explorers, let's get a lay of the land by understanding the essential features of this expansive environment.

Where Data Comes From: Mapping the Sources

Imagine the data universe filled with countless stars, each a unique source of data. Let's survey the prominent types:

- **Internal Data:** This data originates from within an organization, providing invaluable insights into operations and customer behavior:
    - **Customer Relationship Management (CRM) Systems:** A treasure trove of customer interactions, contact information, and purchase history.
    - **Enterprise Resource Planning (ERP) Systems:** Tracking supply chains, inventory management, and financial data flows.
    - **Marketing Automation Systems:** Detailed records of email campaigns, lead generation, and website interactions.
- **External Data:** This data flows from outside your organization, enriching your understanding of the broader world:
    - **Open Government Data:** Freely available datasets covering demographics, weather, scientific research, and more.

- ○ **Syndicated Market Data:** Reports and analyses available for purchase from specialized research companies.
- ○ **Web Scraping:** Extracting structured information from websites, often used for competitor analysis or price monitoring.
- ○ **Social Listening:** Analyzing social media conversations for sentiment analysis, brand monitoring, and trendspotting.

Big Data: The Colossal Star Cluster

Within the data universe, you'll encounter a celestial giant known as Big Data. Its defining characteristics are:

- **Volume:** The immense scale, reaching petabytes or even exabytes of information.
- **Velocity:** The rapid generation of data, particularly with real-time streaming from sensors, financial transactions, or social media feeds.
- **Variety:** An incredible diversity of data formats, from structured numbers and text to unstructured images, videos, and audio.
- **Veracity:** Ensuring the trustworthiness and reliability of data, as quality issues become more prominent with Big Data.

The Habitats of Data Storage

Data needs somewhere to reside, let's explore the different types of data dwellings:

- **Databases:** Highly organized for targeted retrieval, they come in various flavors:
  - ○ **Relational Databases:** Excel's older and wiser cousin, where data is related into tables with rows and columns.

- o **NoSQL Databases:** More flexible for a variety of data, handling large, unstructured datasets.
- **Data Warehouses:** Archives built for analysis, storing vast volumes of historical data for identifying long-term trends.
- **Data Lakes:** Less-structured pools, accepting raw data in all its forms – a data scientist's playground.
- **Cloud Storage:** Like renting a space that grows as you need it, cloud services offer scalable and cost-effective storage options.

Data Governance: Upholding Cosmic Law and Order

With all this data, we need guidelines to ensure its integrity, responsible use, and compliance with regulations:

- **Data Quality:** Maintaining accuracy, completeness, and consistency across the data universe.
- **Data Security:** Protecting data from breaches, theft, and unauthorized access through encryption and access controls.
- **Data Privacy:** Respecting individuals and complying with regulations like GDPR when handling personal information.
- **Data Ethics:** Using data responsibly, addressing bias, ensuring fairness, and considering the societal impacts of analysis.

Chart Your Course in the Data Universe

The data universe awaits your exploration! The rest of this book will be your astrogation guide, providing skills and knowledge for a successful journey.

Additional Resources

- **Types of Data Sources: Explained with Examples**
  https://www.analyticsvidhya.com/blog/2021/04/types-of-data-sources-explained-with-examples/

- **The Beginner's Guide to Data Governance**
  https://www.talend.com/resources/what-is-data-governance/

Section 2:
Nurturing Data Skills and Roles

Crafting the Data Professional: Skills and Roles Explored

The field of data analytics is like a vast and ever-evolving landscape filled with diverse opportunities. In this chapter, we'll take a closer look at the skills that make a successful data professional and explore the different roles available for anyone passionate about unlocking the power of data.

The Essential Skills of the Data Professional

The data professional needs a diverse skillset spanning technical expertise, analytical thinking, and communication abilities. Let's break it down into key areas:

1. **Technical Skills:**
   - **Data Manipulation:** Proficiency in working with spreadsheets (e.g., Excel, Google Sheets) and database tools for data querying and cleaning.
   - **Statistical Analysis:** Understanding key statistical concepts, applying techniques for summarizing and interpreting data.

- ○ **Programming:** At least one general-purpose programming language (e.g., Python, R) for data handling and modeling.
- ○ **Visualization:** The ability to create visualizations (charts, graphs, dashboards) that communicate insights clearly.

2. **Analytical Mindset:**
   - ○ **Problem-solving:** The ability to break complex questions into smaller, addressable components.
   - ○ **Critical Thinking:** Challenging assumptions, evaluating evidence, and uncovering hidden patterns.
   - ○ **Curiosity:** A genuine fascination with data and the stories it can reveal.
   - ○ **Attention to Detail:** Meticulous care for accuracy throughout the analysis process helps ensure correct results.

3. **Communication & Collaboration:**
   - ○ **Data Storytelling:** Translating complex data findings into actionable insights that captivate the audience.
   - ○ **Collaboration:** Working effectively with diverse teams including stakeholders, developers, and analysts.
   - ○ **Domain Knowledge:** Understanding the specific business context or field to maximize data's potential impact.

Shaping Your Data Role: Popular Titles You'll Encounter

The realm of data analytics encompasses a wide range of specializations and titles. Here are some of the most common ones:

- **Data Analyst:** The backbone of analysis, delving into data preparation, exploration, visualization, and answering key business questions.

- **Data Scientist:** Leverages more advanced statistical methods and machine learning algorithms to build predictive and prescriptive models.
- **Data Engineer:** Architects of data infrastructure, building pipelines to collect, store, process, and make data accessible for analysis.
- **Business Intelligence (BI) Analyst:** Focuses on reporting, dashboarding, and providing actionable insights to decision-makers.
- **Database Administrator (DBA):** Manages and maintains databases, ensuring integrity, security, and optimal performance.

The Path is Yours to Forge

It's important to remember that these roles often overlap. Don't get bogged down by rigid titles. Focus on the skills that excite you and consider various roles as stepping stones toward your ideal data career.

Continuous Learning: Your Journey Has No Finish Line

The field of data analysis is constantly evolving. To stay ahead of the curve, successful data professionals adopt these habits:

- **Never stop learning:** Take online courses, read industry blogs, attend workshops to expand your skillset and stay updated.
- **Network with peers:** Engage in data communities to share knowledge, collaborate, and learn about new opportunities.
- **Build a portfolio:** Showcase your expertise through projects and analysis, highlighting your ability to solve real-world problems.

Additional Resources:

- **Data Science Career Guide: Build Your Career in Data Science**
  https://www.springboard.com/guides/data-science-career-guide/
- **Skills Needed to be a Data Analyst: A Comprehensive list**
  https://www.springboard.com/blog/data-analytics/data-analyst-skills/

The Data Professional's Toolkit: Essential Skills Unveiled

In the previous chapter, we explored the diverse roles within the data analytics landscape. Now, let's dive deeper into the essential skills that will equip you for success in these exciting roles. Think of these skills as your trusty companions on your journey through the world of data.

Skill Category 1: Data Wrangling and Manipulation

Data rarely arrives in a perfectly clean and ready-to-analyze package. Mastering these skills will help you tidy up messy data:

- **Spreadsheets:** Excel, Google Sheets, or similar tools are your go-to companions for manipulating data, especially at smaller scales. Know your way around formulas, functions (like VLOOKUP, SUMIF), and pivot tables.
- **SQL:** Structured Query Language is the standard for interacting with relational databases. Learn to extract specific data, join tables, and perform aggregations.
- **Data Cleaning and Preprocessing:** Fixing errors, handling missing values, converting data types, and normalizing datasets are all crucial steps in this stage.

Skill Category 2: Statistical Analysis

A solid foundation in statistics is crucial to interpreting data and drawing informed conclusions. Key concepts include:

- **Descriptive Statistics:** Using measures like mean, median, standard deviation, and visualizations (histograms, box plots) to summarize and describe the key features of a dataset.

- **Inferential Statistics:** Applying techniques like hypothesis testing and confidence intervals to generalize insights from samples to broader populations.
- **Basic Regression:** Understanding different regression models (linear, logistic) helps in identifying relationships and dependencies between variables.

Skill Category 3: Programming

At least one programming language is a key tool for data exploration, modeling, and automating workflows. Python and R are popular choices for data analysis:

- **Python:** A versatile, general-purpose language with powerful data science libraries like Pandas, NumPy, Scikit-learn.
- **R:** Designed specifically for statistical analysis and visualization with packages like dplyr, ggplot2, and Shiny.
- **Programming Basics:** Grasping data types, variables, control flow (loops, conditionals), and functions will help you automate tasks more effectively.

Skill Category 4: Data Visualization

Turning data into effective visuals is a powerful skill, enabling clear communication of trends, patterns, and key insights.

- **Visualization Tools:** Explore popular tools like Tableau, Power BI, or open-source libraries like ggplot2 (in R) or Seaborn (in Python).
- **Visualization Principles:** Understand different chart types (bar charts, scatter plots, line graphs) and when to use them. Learn best practices for visual design, color use, and labeling.

Skill Category 5: Machine Learning (Optional but Highly Valued)

While not a requirement for all data roles, familiarity with machine learning opens doors to advanced problem-solving:

- **Key Algorithms:** Understand the basics of supervised and unsupervised learning algorithms (e.g., decision trees, linear regression, clustering).
- **Machine Learning Libraries:** Get familiar with Scikit-learn (Python) or caret (R) to implement and evaluate models.
- **Understanding Limitations:** It's crucial to know when *not* to use machine learning, recognizing its limitations and the importance of explainability.

Beyond Technical Skills: The Power of Soft Skills

- **Communication:** Clearly articulate findings, explain complex ideas simply, and tailor insights to your audience – key for influencing decisions.
- **Problem-solving:** Break down complex problems into smaller, manageable steps. Develop a logical approach to find solutions.
- **Domain knowledge:** Understand the specific industry where you are applying your data skills to make meaningful contributions to your organization.

Continuous Learning is Key

Remember, technology and techniques evolve rapidly. Stay adaptable and commit to ongoing learning!

Additional Resources

- **Khan Academy: Statistics and Probability** (https://www.khanacademy.org/math/statistics-probability)
- **DataCamp: Intro to Python for Data Science** ([https://www.datacamp.com/courses/intro-to-python-for-data-science])

- **DataCamp: Intro to R for Data Science** ([https://www.datacamp.com/courses/introduction-to-r])
- **The Data Visualisation Catalogue** (Choose the right chart type!) (https://www.datavizcatalogue.com/)

Data Leadership: Guiding the Way in a Data-Driven World

While much of data analysis focuses on individual skills, true data-driven success relies on strong leadership. In this chapter, we'll discuss the qualities of a data leader, the challenges they address, and how they pave the way for organizations to thrive in a data-centric world.

What is Data Leadership?

Data leaders are more than just expert analysts. They are visionaries and strategists who:

- **Build a Data-Driven Culture:** Create an environment where data is valued, trusted, and used at all levels of an organization, going beyond just the analytics team.
- **Align Data Strategy with Business Goals:** Ensure that data initiatives are not isolated projects, but directly support the organization's broader objectives.
- **Champion Data Literacy:** Empower the organization by encouraging data fluency throughout, providing training programs and support.
- **Promote Ethical Data Use:** Establish guidelines and principles for responsible and transparent data handling.

Key Qualities of a Data Leader

Besides technical understanding, a successful data leader embodies several crucial qualities:

- **Communication & Storytelling:** Translating data insights into compelling narratives that influence action and win over stakeholders.

- **Curiosity & Insight:** Asking the right questions, guiding exploration, and uncovering those powerful hidden insights.
- **Strategic Vision:** Seeing the big picture and understanding how data can drive innovation, optimization, and long-term success.
- **Change Management:** Implementing new data practices can meet resistance. Data leaders navigate those challenges, fostering a smooth transition.

The Challenges they Face

The path of a data leader is not without obstacles. Common challenges include:

- **Data Quality:** Ensuring data is accurate, complete, and trustworthy can be an uphill battle, especially in organizations with legacy systems.
- **Data Silos:** Often, data is fragmented across departments. Leaders break down these silos to create a unified view.
- **Legacy Mindsets:** Shifting to a truly data-driven culture might require overcoming resistance or ingrained habits.
- **Skills Shortages:** Building a strong data team may be difficult in a competitive talent market.

The Role of the Chief Data Officer (CDO)

In larger organizations, the role of the Chief Data Officer (CDO) has emerged. This senior executive focuses on:

- **Overall Data Strategy:** Setting the organization-wide vision for how data is collected, managed, and used.
- **Governance Frameworks:** Establishing policies for data security, privacy, and ethical practices.
- **Building Data Infrastructure:** Overseeing investment in the right technologies to support data needs.

Cultivating a Data-Driven Culture

Data leaders are crucial catalysts for a successful data-driven transformation:

- **Start Small, Show Success:** Begin with pilot projects with tangible results to build trust and enthusiasm.
- **Collaboration is Key:** Foster open channels between the data team, business units, and stakeholders.
- **Celebrate Data Wins:** Recognize successes in leveraging data for better decisions, highlighting the value it brings.

Additional Resources

- **What it Takes to be a Data Leader**
  https://hbr.org/2021/05/what-it-takes-to-be-a-data-leader
- **The Emerging Role of the Chief Data Officer**
  https://www.mckinsey.com/business-functions/mckinsey-digital/our-insights/the-emerging-role-of-the-chief-data-officer

Beyond the Analyst: Diverse Roles in the Data Ecosystem

While the title "Data Analyst" is the most familiar, the world of data offers a vast and vibrant array of interconnected careers. Let's explore some roles that your data journey might lead you toward, each leveraging those core data analysis skills in unique ways.

Key Roles Supporting the Data Journey

1. **Data Engineer:** These infrastructure architects build the pipelines, databases, and systems that make data flow smoothly. They focus on scalability, reliability, and making data accessible for others. Skills emphasized are:
   - Database design (SQL and NoSQL)
   - Cloud computing platforms (e.g., AWS, Azure)
   - Big data technologies (e.g., Hadoop, Spark)
2. **Database Administrator (DBA):** The custodians of data storage, they ensure databases run smoothly, are secure, and optimized for performance. Key areas include:
   - Database management systems (e.g., MySQL, Oracle, PostgreSQL)
   - Backup and recovery procedures
   - Performance tuning and optimization
3. **Business Intelligence (BI) Developer:** Focused on dashboards, reports, and visualizations, they translate data into actionable insights for key decision-makers. Skills emphasized are:
   - BI tools (e.g., Power BI, Tableau, Qlik)
   - Data Warehousing and ETL (Extract, Transform, Load) processes
   - Understanding of business KPIs (Key Performance Indicators)

Specializations Using Advanced Skills

4. **Data Scientist:** Data scientists dive into advanced analytics, machine learning, and predictive modeling. Core competencies include:
   - Strong foundation in statistics and mathematics
   - Machine learning algorithms and model evaluation
   - Programming in Python or R, plus libraries like Scikit-learn and TensorFlow
5. **Machine Learning Engineer:** Focused on the practical implementation of machine learning models. They build and deploy models into production systems. Skills needed are:
   - Model deployment (e.g., Flask, AWS SageMaker)
   - Software engineering principles for robust code
   - Proficiency in a programming language like Python
6. **Data Architect:** These big-picture thinkers design the overall blueprint for an organization's data management systems, considering future growth and integration needs. Skills they focus on:
   - Data modeling and system design principles
   - Understanding of various data technologies
   - Ability to align data architecture with business goals

Emerging & Niche Roles

- **Data Security Specialist:** As data grows, so does the importance of protecting it. They design and implement security measures like encryption, access controls, and threat detection.
- **Data Ethicist:** Responsible use of data is paramount. They advise organizations on ethical implications of data collection and analysis, ensuring fairness and preventing potential biases.
- **Data Journalist:** Experts at unearthing compelling stories within datasets and communicating them to the public through impactful visualizations and narratives.

Remember: Fluidity is Key!

The data landscape constantly evolves, and roles often have overlapping skills. Don't feel confined to a single title. Your path may see you move between these various roles!

Additional Resources

- **10 Types of Data Science Jobs and Their Roles in the Company**
  https://www.springboard.com/blog/data-science/data-scienc e-jobs/
- **Beyond the Data Scientist: 12 Roles for Data-Obsessed Professionals**
  https://www.forbes.com/sites/louiscolumbus/2021/08/09/bey ond-the-data-scientist-12-roles-for-data-obsessed-professio nals/?sh=3c8571f44bb8

Section 3:
Mapping the Landscape of Analytics Tools

Charting the Course: Exploring Analytics Tool Categories

The vast world of analytics tools can feel overwhelming for a beginner. This chapter serves as your compass, guiding you through the major categories of tools you'll encounter on your data journey.

Category 1: Spreadsheets

- **Tools:** Microsoft Excel, Google Sheets, LibreOffice Calc
- **Strengths:** The first stop for many analysts. Great for data cleaning, manipulation, basic calculations, and charts.
- **Best for:** Smaller datasets, quick analysis, and ad-hoc tasks. Users already familiar with spreadsheets will find a smooth entry point.

Category 2: Data Visualization and BI Tools

- **Tools:** Tableau, Power BI, Qlik Sense, Looker
- **Strengths:** Design interactive dashboards, reports, and stunning visualizations, ideal for conveying insights to stakeholders.

- **Best for:** Sharing results across the organization, regular monitoring of KPIs (Key Performance Indicators), and identifying patterns that might be hidden in tables.

Category 3: Statistical Analysis and Programming Environments

- **Tools:** R, Python, SAS, SPSS, MATLAB
- **Strengths:** Immense flexibility for statistical analysis, modeling, and custom data solutions. Often open-source (free!) with large communities for support.
- **Best for:** Going deep with statistics, predictive modeling, machine learning, and automating analysis for repeatable tasks.

Category 4: Database Management Tools

- **Tools:** MySQL Workbench, SQLite, PostgreSQL, Microsoft SQL Server Management Studio
- **Strengths:** Working directly with databases. Creating tables, writing queries (with SQL), and managing access/permissions.
- **Best for:** Extracting specific data, joining information from multiple sources, and tasks requiring direct database interaction.

Category 5: Big Data Tools

- **Tools:** Apache Hadoop, Apache Spark, Kafka, NoSQL databases (MongoDB, Cassandra)
- **Strengths:** Designed for massive datasets that don't fit the mold of traditional databases. Handle distributed storage and processing.
- **Best for:** Working with petabytes of data, real-time streaming analytics, and working with large, unstructured datasets.

Category 6: Cloud-Based Analytics Platforms

- **Tools:** Amazon Web Services (AWS), Microsoft Azure, Google Cloud Platform
- **Strengths:** Scalability – pay only for what you use. Often include a suite of data tools: storage, databases, analytics services, and machine learning solutions.
- **Best for:** Organizations moving to the cloud, those needing flexible and cost-effective infrastructure, and accessing advanced AI/ML services.

Factors to Consider (Beyond the Categories)

- **Ease of Use:** Do you need simple drag-and-drop interfaces, or do you enjoy the power of coding?
- **Collaboration Features:** How will you share results and work with your team?
- **Cost:** Ranges from free (open-source) to enterprise licenses with extensive support. Many tools offer free trials to explore.
- **Integration:** How easily does the tool fit with your existing data systems and workflows?

It's Not One-Tool-Fits-All

A skilled data professional often uses a combination of tools, each chosen for a specific task within the broader analysis process.

Additional Resources

- **Gartner Magic Quadrant for Analytics and Business Intelligence Platforms**
  https://www.gartner.com/en/research/market-guides/magic-quadrant-analytics-business-intelligence
- **Top 15 Data Analytics Tools to Consider**
  https://www.simplilearn.com/data-analytics-tools-article

Ready to take a closer look at how to choose the right tool for the job? Let's dive into 'Tool Selection Demystified' in the next chapter!

Tool Selection Demystified: Navigating the Options

The world of data analytics tools is vast and ever-evolving. Choosing wisely empowers you on your data journey. Think of this chapter as your compass – let's break down the decision-making process and find those hidden gems within the diverse tool landscape.

Know Your Destination: Start with the Fundamentals

Before diving into tool comparisons, take a moment for introspection:

- **The Core Problem:** Clearly define the business question you're tackling or the process you want to improve. Understanding the "why" behind your analysis will help narrow down tool options.
- **Data, Data Everywhere:** Assess the size, variety (structured vs. unstructured), and real-time needs. A small spreadsheet-friendly dataset has vastly different needs than terabytes of streaming sensor data.
- **Your Skills, Your Preference:** Are you comfortable with code, or do you prefer drag-and-drop interfaces? Matching tools to your skillset maximizes efficiency and learning potential.
- **Desired Deliverables:** Do you need to communicate insights visually through dashboards, or do in-depth statistical reports drive decisions? Knowing your desired outcome helps pinpoint tools with the right strengths.
- **Budgetary Constraints:** Balancing your needs with the reality of cost is important. Be aware of initial purchase prices, ongoing subscription fees, and potential training costs associated with certain tools.

- **The Power of Collaboration:** Will this be a solo adventure, or do you need tools that facilitate teamwork and seamless sharing of work?

Evaluating Your Suitcase: Factors to Consider

Let's unpack the key features to consider when selecting your tool-arsenal:

- **Functionality Does Matter:** Ensure the tool aligns with your specific analytical needs. Prioritize tools that excel in your required areas, whether that's visualization, statistical analysis, or machine learning model building.
- **Learning Curve:** Can you hit the ground running, or will training be necessary? Factor in potential time spent on learning new a tool – it's a worthy investment but needs to be considered as part of your project timeline.
- **Compatibility Check:** Can the tool easily access, process, and integrate with your existing data sources and technology infrastructure?
- **Scaling With You:** Be future-focused. Consider if the tool can grow with you as your datasets become larger and your analysis more complex.
- **The Community Factor:** Especially for open-source tools, a vibrant community translates to readily available help, documentation, and potential custom solutions created by others.
- **Pricing That Works:** Explore free vs. paid options, upfront purchase costs vs. subscription models, and whether there are "freemium" options with basic functionality before committing fully.

Hands-On Exploration: Test Drives and Prototyping

- **Embrace Trials and Demos:** Many reputable tools offer these, allowing you to directly experience if the tool clicks for you.
- **Your Data, the Star:** The most effective test is using a sample of your own data. Can it be imported easily, and can you perform the necessary manipulations and analysis?
- **Focus on Ease of Use:** Assess how intuitive the interface is and whether it matches your workflow preferences.

The Hidden Considerations

- **Integration Powerhouse:** Your tool should be a team player. Consider if it easily integrates with existing databases, reporting platforms, or other tools you use throughout the analysis journey.
- **Reputable Support:** Investigate the vendor's track record in providing support, good documentation, and having a roadmap for future development
- **Beyond the Desktop: **Consider the deployment options. Do you need a cloud-based solution for accessibility, or will an on-premise installation better suit your company's security policies?

The Multi-Tool Advantage

As you become a data wizard, you'll likely find yourself wielding a combination of tools. An expert data analyst learns the strengths of each and uses them strategically throughout their workflow!

Additional Resources

- **Tool selection guide: How to choose the right data analytics tools**
  https://www.cio.com/article/3236454/tool-selection-guide-how-to-choose-the-right-data-analytics-tools.html
- **How to Choose the Best Data Analytics Tools for Your Problem**

https://www.datapine.com/blog/how-to-choose-the-best-data-analytics-tools-for-your-problem/

Ready for a fun detour? In the next chapter, let's travel through time and explore the 'Evolution of Analytics Tools'!

The Evolution of Analytics Tools: From Past to Present

Data analysis has a rich and fascinating history. Understanding how tools have evolved lets us appreciate the power we wield today. Let's journey through the key eras and technological leaps that transformed how we harness the potential of data.

The Pre-Computer Age: When Paper and Ingenuity Reigned

- **Manual Methods:** For centuries, analyzing data meant meticulous calculations by hand, aided by tools like the abacus or slide rule. Statistics was the domain of specialists, and insights could take weeks or months to surface.
- **Mechanical Marvels:** The early 20th century saw inventions like punch-card tabulating machines, used for tasks like the US Census. These offered some automation but were limited in flexibility.

The Birth of the Digital Spreadsheet: An Analytical Revolution

- **VisiCalc and Beyond:** The advent of personal computers in the 1980s brought pioneering spreadsheets like VisiCalc and Lotus 1-2-3. Suddenly, analysts could digitally organize, perform calculations at lightning speed, and visualize trends through simple charts.
- **Empowering Businesses:** Spreadsheets quickly became integral across industries. Financial modeling, basic reporting, and simple what-if scenarios became accessible to a wider range of professionals.

Specialized Software & Databases: Growth of Analytical Power

- **The Statistical Giants:** SAS, SPSS, and similar programs were developed for serious statistical work. They provided analysts with an arsenal of techniques: regression analysis, hypothesis testing, and in-depth modeling for both research and business uses.
- **Database Dominance:** Relational databases (e.g., Oracle, SQL Server) optimized for efficient storage and retrieval of structured data became the backbone of businesses. SQL became the essential language for interacting with these vast data stores.

The Internet Era: Visualization and Accessibility

- **Visual Revolution:** Tools like Tableau and Qlik brought visually striking dashboards to the mainstream. Business users could now easily track KPIs, spot trends, and share insights without being data experts themselves.
- **Rise of Open-Source:** The power of community-driven languages like R and Python took hold. Their dedicated machine learning and statistical libraries pushed boundaries, offering cost-effective options for complex analysis and custom solutions.
- **Data on the Web:** The internet itself became a massive data source. Web analytics tools emerged to track user behavior, driving growth in digital marketing and optimization.

The Modern Landscape: Big Data, Cloud, and AI Arrive

- **Taming the Big Data Beast:** Facing an explosion of data no longer fitting into tidy rows, tools like Hadoop and Spark innovated. Distributed processing and storage allowed analysis on petabyte scales across vast computing clusters.
- **Cloud Supremacy:** AWS, Azure, and Google Cloud transformed the data landscape. On-demand processing

power, scalable storage, and a suite of AI/Machine Learning tools became accessible to businesses big and small.
- **Low-Code/No-Code Disruption:** Visual-focused tools emerged, empowering even non-programmers to perform complex analysis tasks with drag-and-drop interfaces, and to build predictive models without writing a single line of code.
- **Self-Service Analytics:** Dashboards and data-discovery platforms enable business users to answer their own questions by exploring datasets intuitively, reducing reliance on specialized data analysts for every minor query.

The Future: Where the Journey Takes Us Next

- **AI-Powered Analysts:** Artificial Intelligence will increasingly automate mundane tasks like cleaning data, suggesting optimal visualizations, and flagging anomalies in data flows.
- **Conversational Analytics:** Imagine asking, "Show me last quarter's revenue trends by product category, broken down by region" and getting an instant response – that's the power of Natural Language Processing (NLP) in data interaction.
- **Focus on Explainability:** Trust in AI will hinge on our ability to understand why models make specific predictions. Unraveling the "black box" and ensuring transparent AI are key for responsible use of these powerful tools.

It's Never Been a More Exciting Time!

This ongoing evolution is a testament to human ingenuity. With potent tools at our fingertips, the onus lies on us, as data professionals, to ensure we leverage them ethically, focus on problem-solving, and never stop learning to stay ahead of the curve.

Additional Resources

- **Timeline: The Evolution of Analytics**
  https://www.tableau.com/learn/articles/timeline-evolution-analytics
- **The History (and Future) of Data Visualization**
  https://www.tableau.com/learn/articles/data-visualization

Let's continue the adventure. Our next chapter will demystify the 'Analytics Framework' – your roadmap for turning data into actionable insights!

Section 4:
Exploring the Data Analytics Framework

Unlocking Insights: Delving into the Analytics Framework

Think of the data analytics framework as your treasure map. It provides a structured approach to navigate the journey from raw data to actionable insights that can change the course of your organization. Let's break down this map and explore its key components within the process of data analytics.

The Essential Framework (Simplified)

While there are various frameworks, the core concepts remain universal. Here's a simplified version, which we'll expand on shortly:

1. **Problem Definition:** Frame the business question you want to address or the challenge you want to understand.
2. **Data Collection:** Gather relevant data from internal sources, external sources, or by conducting new studies and experiments
3. **Data Cleaning and Preparation:** Ensure your data is accurate, complete, and formatted for analysis.

4. **Exploratory Data Analysis (EDA):** Dive into the data, uncover patterns, identify anomalies, form initial hypotheses through visualizations and summary statistics.
5. **Modeling and Analysis:** Choose and apply appropriate modeling techniques (statistics, forecasting, machine learning) to address your question.
6. **Interpretation and Storytelling:** Make sense of your findings, clearly communicate the insights, and suggest recommendations.

It's Often Cyclical, Not Linear

Remember, this framework is an iterative process. Findings in one step might lead you to re-exam earlier data collection, or uncover the need to clean data in a different way. It's a guided adventure, not a rigid checklist.

Expanding on the Core Steps

Let's explore each step in more detail:

1. **Problem Definition**
   - Clarity is vital. Broad questions like, "How can we improve sales?" will lead to unfocused analysis.
   - Be specific. For example: "Identify the primary factors influencing customer churn in the last quarter."
2. **Data Collection**
   - What data is already available? (Sales records, website logs, social media feedback, etc.)
   - Can it answer your research question? Is the quality sufficient?
   - Do you need to collect new data through surveys, experiments, or external sources?
3. **Data Cleaning and Preparation**

- Dealing with missing values, inconsistencies (different date formats), and possible outliers.
- Transform data into the necessary formats (e.g., combining columns, text normalization)
- This step can be incredibly time-consuming, but a well-prepared dataset is crucial for meaningful results.

4. **Exploratory Data Analysis (EDA)**
   - Using visualizations (histograms, scatter plots, etc.) to summarize and find trends.
   - Calculate basic statistics (mean, median, standard deviation) to understand the data's distribution.
   - Formulate hypotheses - "Do customers from a certain region have higher purchase frequency?"

5. **Modeling and Analysis**
   - Choose techniques aligned with your questions and desired outcome:
     - Descriptive (summary statistics)
     - Diagnostic (correlation analysis)
     - Predictive (regression models, time series forecasting)
     - Prescriptive (optimization techniques)

6. **Interpretation and Storytelling**
   - Translate complex findings into simple, compelling narratives.
   - Visualizations are your powerful allies – choose the right charts for clarity!
   - Don't just report the numbers - provide context: Why does this matter to the business?

Additional Resources

- **CRISP-DM: A Popular Framework**
  https://www.datasciencecentral.com/profiles/blogs/crisp-dm-a-standard-methodology-to-ensure-a-good-outcome

- **Introduction to the Data Science Process**
  https://towardsdatascience.com/introduction-to-the-data-science-process-a9a5db943f39

Ready to dig deeper? In the next chapter, we'll unpack the 'Three Pillars of Data Analytics' that support this entire framework!

The Three Pillars of Data Analytics: A Detailed Exploration

Successful data analysis rests upon three fundamental pillars that ensure you derive valid and impactful insights. Whether you are a budding analyst or a seasoned professional, understanding these pillars is essential as they guide your actions throughout your data analytics journey.

Pillar 1: Descriptive Analytics - Understanding the Past

- **Mission:** Descriptive analytics tells you "what happened." It involves summarizing historical data to find trends, patterns, and key metrics.
- **Essential Tools:**
    - Aggregations (sum, count, average, etc.)
    - Visualizations (bar charts, line graphs, histograms)
    - Pivot Tables (for easy cross-tabulations)
- **Example Questions It Answers:**
    - What were the total sales last quarter?
    - Which product category is the most popular?
    - Has website traffic increased over the last year?
- **Foundation for Further Analysis:** It provides a baseline understanding, but we want to go deeper.

Pillar 2: Diagnostic Analytics - Explaining the "Why"

- **Mission:** Diagnostic analytics digs into the causes behind the trends identified by descriptive analysis. The goal is to understand "why" something happened.
- **Techniques Used:**
    - Correlation Analysis: Identifying relationships between variables.

- Hypothesis Testing: Testing assumptions about what might drive outcomes.
- Root Cause Analysis: Drilling down to find the underlying factors.
- **Example Questions It Answers:**
  - Why did sales decline in a specific region?
  - What factors influence customer satisfaction?
  - Why did a marketing campaign underperform?
- **Deeper Insights:** Diagnostic analytics helps us go beyond the surface-level observations.

Pillar 3: Predictive & Prescriptive Analytics – Foreseeing the Future

Predictive Analytics

- **Mission:** Using historical data to forecast future outcomes and potential trends. It's about anticipating "what might happen".
- **Key Techniques:**
  - Regression Analysis: Modeling the relationship between variables to predict values.
  - Time-Series Forecasting: Analyzing data over time to predict trends.
  - Machine Learning Models: Learning from patterns to make predictions about new data (e.g., decision trees, neural networks).
- **Example Questions It Answers:**
  - What is the projected customer churn for the next quarter?
  - How much inventory will we need to meet next month's demand?
  - Which customers are most likely to respond to a new offer?

Prescriptive Analytics

- **Mission:** Goes beyond predicting to suggest optimal courses of action. It aims to answer "what should we do about it."
- **Techniques Involved:**
  - Optimization Techniques: Finding the best solution given constraints.
  - Simulation Modeling: Building models to test different scenarios.
  - Machine Learning-based Recommendations: Suggesting actions based on vast data patterns.
- **Example Questions It Answers:**
  - How should we adjust pricing to maximize profit?
  - What's the optimal inventory allocation for our warehouses?
  - Which marketing channel should we invest in for the highest return?

The Power of Combining the Pillars

The most valuable insights often emerge by weaving these pillars together:

1. **Descriptive:** Observe a decline in product sales.
2. **Diagnostic:** Discover the decline is linked to increased competitor activity.
3. **Predictive:** Project that the decline will continue unless action is taken.
4. **Prescriptive:** Model the best pricing strategy or promotional campaign to regain market share considering various factors.

Additional Resources

- **Descriptive, Predictive, Prescriptive Analytics Explained** https://www.sisense.com/glossary/descriptive-predictive-prescriptive-analytics/

- **Data Science for Business [Foster Provost and Tom Fawcett] (Book)** - https://www.amazon.com/Data-Science-Business-Data-Analytic-Thinking/dp/1449361323 (Great resource for the pillars of analytics.)

In the next chapter, we'll see how these pillars, your toolkit, and your strategic thinking intersect to create powerful results! Let's move on to 'The Intersection of Data: Where Tools, Techniques, and Strategy Meet.'

The Intersection of Data: Where Tools, Techniques, and Strategy Meet

Harnessing the true power of data analysis requires more than just knowing individual tools and techniques. Our previous chapters explored the data analytics framework, different tools, and the three pillars of analytics. In this chapter, we'll see how those elements converge to create powerful solutions.

Where the Magic Happens

To unlock the insights hiding within your data, think of this intersection as your analytical engine:

- **Tools:** Your powerful instruments range from spreadsheets to visualization tools and sophisticated machine learning platforms.
- **Techniques:** These are your methods: Statistical analysis, modeling techniques drawn from the three pillars (descriptive, diagnostic, predictive/prescriptive).
- **Strategy:** The guiding force. Your analytical approach must align with the overarching problem you're solving and the business goals you want to achieve.

Example Scenario: Optimizing Product Pricing

Let's illustrate how these elements work together:

Business Problem: Determine the optimal pricing strategy to maximize profit for a product line.

- **Strategy:**

- Understand pricing sensitivity. How does a price change impact sales volume?
- Investigate cost structures and profit margins.
- Consider competitor pricing in the market.
- Aim for the right balance – increasing sales without sacrificing profitability.

- **Tools:**
  - Spreadsheet or Statistical Software: For data cleaning, calculations, and modeling.
  - Database tools: To access sales data, transaction costs, and market data.
  - Visualization tools: To analyze the relationship between price and sales trends.
- **Techniques:**
  - Descriptive Analytics: Summarize past sales at different price points.
  - Correlation Analysis: Understand the relationship between price changes and sales volume.
  - Regression Modeling: Build models to predict demand at various prices.
  - Optimization (Prescriptive): Find the price point that maximizes profit (considering other factors).

It's About Asking the Right Questions

Your strategy will guide the choice of tools and techniques. Some key questions:

- **What questions do I need to answer:** Is it about past performance, forecasting, or recommending ideal actions? This guides the choice of analytic type.
- **Data Format:** Is my data structured for easy calculation or do I need to handle unstructured text (e.g., customer reviews for insights on sentiment)?

- **Deliverable Format:** Are dashboards for monitoring vital, or do I need a research-style report with in-depth statistical findings?

Real-World Considerations

- **Complexity:** Simple problems often need straightforward use of tools. Complex questions might involve a chain of techniques and a mix of tools.
- **Scale:** Small datasets might be tackled in a spreadsheet, while Big Data calls for specialized tools.
- **Automation:** Is this a one-time analysis, or do results need to be regularly refreshed? This impacts the level of automation you build.

The Human Factor

Remember, tools are enablers. It's your analytical thinking that makes the difference:

- **Curiosity:** Ask the questions that lead to deeper understanding of a problem.
- **Critical Thinking:** Don't take data at face value. Challenge your own findings.
- **Contextual Understanding:** Results always need to be interpreted in the context of your business.

Continuous Learning is Key

The data landscape keeps evolving. Stay curious, embrace new tools, explore case studies, and see how others combine techniques to solve real-world problems.

Additional Resources

- **Data Strategy: How to Profit from a World of Big Data, Analytics and the Internet of Things [by Bernard Marr]**

(Book)
https://www.amazon.com/Data-Strategy-Profit-Analytics-Inte
rnet/dp/074947985X

- **Examples of data analysis techniques and how to use them**
  https://www.datasciencecentral.com/profiles/blogs/30-techni
  ques-to-improve-your-data-analysis

Your analytical journey is a continuous one! As you gain experience, you'll discover exciting new ways to make data work for you. Ready for your next step? Let's dive into the diverse world of 'Data Types and Formats'

Section 5:
Demystifying Data Types and Formats

Decoding Data: Types, Files, and Formats Demystified

Think of data as the raw ingredients for making something delicious. Just like a recipe calls for various types of ingredients, successful data analysis depends on understanding the diverse types of data you'll encounter, how they are stored, and how to work with them.

Fundamental Data Types

Let's start by understanding the basic building blocks of data:

1. **Quantitative Data**
   - **Numerical:** Represents measurable quantities. Two main flavors:
     - **Discrete:** Whole numbers (e.g., number of orders placed, survey ratings from 1 to 5)
     - **Continuous:** Can take any value within a range (e.g., temperature, time, weight)
2. **Qualitative Data**
   - **Categorical:** Represents descriptive categories. Two subtypes:

- **Nominal:** Categories with no order (e.g., customer gender, product color)
- **Ordinal:** Categories with ranking (e.g., survey response: Very Satisfied, Satisfied, Neutral)

3. **Structured Data**
   - **Highly Organized:** Easily fits into tables, rows, and columns (spreadsheets, relational databases). Example: A sales transaction table with columns for Order ID, Customer Name, Product, Date, Price.

4. **Unstructured Data**
   - **No Rigid Format:** Text-heavy (e.g., social media posts, emails), images, videos, audio files.
   - **More Analysis Effort:** They often require specialized techniques like text mining or image processing to extract information.

5. **Semi-structured Data**
   - **The Middle Ground:** Have some organization, but not as rigid as tables. Think of data in formats like JSON or XML, which use tags and hierarchies to give data context.

How Data is Stored (File Formats)

Data needs to live somewhere! Common file formats you'll encounter include:

- **Delimited Files:**
  - **CSV (Comma Separated Values):** Plain text where each line represents a row, columns are separated by commas. Simple and widely compatible.
  - **TSV (Tab Separated Values):** Similar to CSV, but uses tabs as the character separating columns.
- **Spreadsheet Formats:**
  - **XLS, XLSX (Microsoft Excel):** Popular but can have size limitations for large datasets.
- **Database Formats:**

- ○ **SQL:** Files often used to backup or export relational database structures.
  - ○ **Proprietary database files:** (e.g., .MDB for MS Access)
- **Structured Text Formats:**
  - ○ **XML (Extensible Markup Language):** Uses tags to add meaning to data (e.g., John Doe)
  - ○ **JSON (JavaScript Object Notation):** Lightweight and very popular for web/API data exchange for its readability.

Why Understanding Types and Formats Matter

- **Tool Compatibility:** The right tool for the job! Spreadsheets are great for smaller structured data, but text analysis or image processing needs specialized tools.
- **Efficient Analysis:** Structured data is usually fastest to analyze. Understanding your data lets you choose the right approach.
- **Data Preparation:** You may need to convert between formats. For instance, messy text data could be cleaned and organized into a structured table format.

Additional Resources

- **Data Types in Data Analytics: A Comprehensive Overview**
  https://www.sciencedirect.com/topics/computer-science/data-type
- **Introduction to Common File Formats**
  https://www.techwalla.com/articles/introduction-to-common-file-formats

Ready to take a closer look at the specific formatting languages that give data structure? Let's move onto 'The Language of Data: Understanding Formats and Structures'.

The Language of Data: Understanding Formats and Structures

In the previous chapter, we explored basic data types and file formats. Now, let's go deeper by understanding how formats add structure and meaning to your raw data, making it machine-readable and easier to analyze. Think of these formats as different languages that data can speak.

Key Formats for Structured Data

1. **CSV (Comma Separated Values)**
- **The Simplicity Champion:** Plain text format where commas separate values (columns). Great for quick readability and data exchange.

Example:
Order ID, Customer Name, Product, Price
1001, Sarah Lee, Widget A, $24.99
1002, John Baker, Gadget B, $15.50

•

2. **Spreadsheets (Excel)**
- **The Visual Workspace:** Data organized in grids. Intuitive, but has limitations in handling very large datasets.
- **Behind the Scenes:** While appearing simple to use, spreadsheet files store data, formatting, and formulas in a structured way.
3. **Relational Databases**
- **Organized Powerhouse:** Data structured into tables with rows and columns. Relationships between tables are defined, allowing for complex queries.

- **Language of Databases:** SQL (Structured Query Language) is essential to interact with relational databases.

Formats for Semi-Structured Data

1. **XML (Extensible Markup Language)**
- **Flexible Labeling:** Uses tags to describe data, adding context and hierarchy.
- **Example:**

```
<customer>
  <name>Alice Johnson</name>
  <email>alice@example.com</email>
  <order id="12345">
    <item>Book A</item>
    <price>19.99</price>
  </order>
</customer>
```

2. **JSON (JavaScript Object Notation)**
- **Web-Friendly Favorite:** Popular for web APIs and data exchange. Lightweight and easy to read for both humans and machines.
- **Example:**

```
{
  "customer": {
    "name": "Alice Johnson",
    "email": "alice@example.com",
    "order": {
      "id": "12345",
      "item": "Book A",
      "price": 19.99
    }
  }
}
```

When to Choose Which

- **Structured for Speed:** For analysis within spreadsheets or databases, CSV or similar delimited formats are easy to import.
- **Flexibility & Portability:** XML and JSON excel when you need to represent more complex data and move it between systems.
- **Web Data:** JSON rules the world of data passed through web applications and APIs.

Demystifying Unstructured Data

Unstructured data (text, images, audio, video) pose unique challenges. Here's where some specialized techniques come in:

- **Text Mining & Natural Language Processing (NLP):** Extracting insights, identifying sentiment, and classifying text documents.
- **Image and Video Analysis:** Computer vision for object recognition, pattern detection, etc.

Additional Resources

- **Learn XML basics** (https://www.w3schools.com/xml/)
- **JSON Tutorial** (https://www.w3schools.com/js/js_json_intro.asp)

Understanding how data is structured is essential for successful analysis. In our next chapter, let's explore 'Data Diversity' and how to handle a wide range of data sources for a holistic view!

Data Diversity: Navigating the Multifaceted World of Data

The data landscape is a vibrant ecosystem, teeming with information in many shapes and sizes. To unlock the most potent insights, a skilled analyst learns to navigate this rich and varied terrain. Let's explore common data sources, the challenges they bring, and how to harness their combined strength for a 360-degree view.

Internal Sources: The Heart of Your Business

These are the data arteries running within your organization:

- **Databases & CRMs:** Your treasure trove of customer information, sales transactions, and operational data live here. Often found in well-structured relational databases making analysis (relatively) smooth sailing.
- **Spreadsheets:** While sometimes dismissed as messy, they contain a wealth of departmental-level information. Budgets, project trackers, and experiment results – these are often diamonds in the rough, if you know where to look.
- **Financial Systems:** Accounting software holds the pulse of your business. Analyzing revenue, expenses, and cash flow trends paints a detailed picture of your financial health and allows for optimization.
- **Web Analytics:** Understanding your website traffic is akin to reading the minds of your potential customers. How users navigate, where they linger, and where they drop off are invaluable for crafting online experiences that convert.
- **Marketing Automation:** Tools like email platforms track the entire campaign journey: open rates, clicks, conversions. Integrating this with sales data shows you precisely where

leads fall out of your funnel, allowing for targeted improvements.

External Sources: See the Bigger Picture

Don't limit yourself to your own data backyard! The wider world holds valuable insights:

- **Open Government Data:** A wealth of information on demographics, economic indicators, weather patterns, and more is freely available. Understanding these larger trends helps you see how your business fits into the global context. (https://www.data.gov/)
- **Market Research Reports:** Sometimes an investment is worthwhile. These reports provide curated data and analysis on specific industries, helping you benchmark your performance, see upcoming trends, and spot new opportunities.
- **Social Media Listening:** The real-time, unfiltered voice of the consumer is on social media. Tools for sentiment analysis and trend spotting help you gauge brand perception, identify pain points, and even predict shifts in customer behavior.
- **Web Scraping:** When readily available datasets don't exist, ethical web scraping can be your secret tool. Extract product information for comparison, gather reviews for competitor analysis… the possibilities abound, but use it responsibly and with respect to websites' terms of service.

Unstructured Data: Where the Real Challenge (and Potential) Lies

- **Textual Data:** The treasure chest is vast, yet the gems are hidden. Customer reviews, survey responses, call transcripts, and even old emails contain a wealth of qualitative insights. Natural Language Processing (NLP) techniques are essential to analyze this type of data, transforming words into quantifiable sentiment and themes.

- **Images and Videos:** Visual data has exploded in the digital age. Computer vision techniques allow you to analyze product images for trends, monitor security footage for anomalies, or even track crowd sentiment in real-time.
- **Sensor Data (IoT):** The Internet of Things generates a firehose of real-time data. Monitoring machine health, optimizing energy usage, and providing predictive maintenance are just a few examples of how IoT data can revolutionize your operations.

The Challenge of Mastering Diversity

- **Varied Formats:** CSV, JSON, XML, raw text, images – knowing how to ingest and transform data from different formats is a core skill.
- **Inconsistent Quality:** External data, collected for multiple purposes, might not adhere to your internal quality standards. Be prepared to spend extra time cleaning and verifying.
- **Volume and Velocity:** Social media or IoT data streams are vast and fast-moving. This might necessitate Big Data tools (Hadoop, Spark) to handle and process them effectively.
- **Legal and Ethical Considerations:** Always ensure data from external sources is acquired and used ethically. Laws like GDPR regulate personal data usage, so be sure to stay informed.

The Power of Combining Data Streams

The true magic lies in combining diverse data sources:

- **360-Degree Customer View:** Match web analytics with CRM data, adding an extra layer of context to those anonymous website visitors. This lets you tailor their experience.

- **Competitive Analysis:** Scraped product data from competitors, combined with market research, gives you a detailed landscape of your competitive position.
- **Predicting the Unpredictable:** External factors, seemingly disconnected, might hold the key to forecasting. Analyze weather trends alongside seasonal sales data for powerful predictive models.

Additional Resources

- **7 Main Types of Data Sources | With Examples**
  https://www.analyticsvidhya.com/blog/2021/11/7-main-types-of-data-sources-with-examples/
- **Unstructured Data: The Data Type That's Everywhere**
  https://www.datanami.com/2018/11/28/unstructured-data-the-data-type-thats-everywhere/
- **Open Data Handbook** (https://opendatahandbook.org/) – Excellent resource for everything about open data

Welcome the complexity of data diversity – it's where unique breakthroughs await! Let's move on to the next exciting step: 'The Journey Begins: Tracing Data from Collection'.

Section 6:
Tracing Data Pathways: From Collection to Analysis

The Journey Begins: Tracing Data from Collection

Data analysis is often likened to a journey, and the first step is always finding out where your data originates. Understanding the various ways data is generated and collected is crucial because it impacts its quality and the insights you may be able to derive.

Common Sources of Data

Let's explore the major pathways data takes to arrive at your fingertips:

1. **Manual Entry:**
   - **Surveys & Forms:** Structured question-and-answer formats allow for controlled data collection and easier analysis. Tools like Google Forms or SurveyMonkey streamline this process.
   - **Direct Input:** Data entry personnel often enter information into databases or systems. Prone to human error, so extra vigilance is needed to ensure data quality.
2. **Transactional Systems:**

- CRM Systems: Every customer interaction—sales calls, orders placed, support tickets – leaves a digital footprint in the CRM.
- E-commerce Platforms: Track online purchases, browsing behavior, and product preferences. A goldmine for understanding consumer behavior.
- Point-of-Sale (POS) Systems: Capture detailed sales data and inventory movement in brick-and-mortar retail settings.

3. Sensors and IoT Devices:
   - Manufacturing Machinery: Sensors monitor equipment performance, temperature, vibration – allowing predictive maintenance and optimization.
   - Smart Homes & Wearables: Collect real-time data like temperature, energy usage, or fitness metrics, providing insights for optimization and personalization.
   - Logistics: GPS tracking for fleets and individual packages gives real-time visibility into supply chain efficiency.

4. Web Scraping:
   - Purposeful Extraction: Automated scripts pull specific data, like product prices from competitors' sites or reviews from social media. (Note: Always respect terms of use for websites, and prioritize ethical scraping practices.)

5. APIs (Application Programming Interfaces):
   - Interconnected Systems: APIs forge 'digital highways'. They allow your tools to "talk" to other systems, pulling in data in real-time (e.g., weather data for an agriculture analytics app).
   - Social Media: APIs allow you to collect and analyze social media data on specific topics, brands, or sentiments.

6. Existing Datasets:

- o **Open Data Repositories:** Government data, scientific studies, and research datasets can be invaluable for certain analyses. (https://www.data.gov/)
- o **Market Research Syndicators:** Paid services provide curated data and analysis within specific industries.

Considerations Affecting Data Quality

- **Collection Method:** Manual processes are more prone to errors versus automated ones.
- **Timeliness:** Stale data loses its value quickly! Is it real-time (sensor data) or periodic updates (surveys)?
- **Bias:** How the data is collected can introduce bias. Are survey respondents representative of your actual audience? Do sensors have measurement drift that needs correction?
- **Completeness:** Missing data is a common challenge. Understanding *why* it's missing is crucial for responsible analysis.

The Importance of Data Lineage

Think of this as your data's family tree. Tracing data lineage means:

- **Understanding Transformations:** As data moves, it may be aggregated, cleaned, or combined with other data. This history impacts how you can interpret results.
- **Troubleshooting Issues:** When anomalies surface, data lineage helps you trace them back to the source. Was it a sensor malfunction or an improper calculation along the way?
- **Compliance:** Regulations may require you to prove the origins of data and how it was handled – data lineage is non-negotiable.

Additional Resources

- **6 Common Data Collection Methods (With Examples and Tools)**
  https://www.formpl.us/blog/data-collection-methods
- **The Importance of Data Lineage**
  https://www.dataversity.net/the-importance-of-data-lineage/

Ready to embark deeper into the transformation stage? In the next chapter, 'The Analytical Odyssey: Exploring Data Transformation', we'll tackle cleaning, shaping, and preparing data for the rigors of analysis!

The Analytical Odyssey: Exploring Data Transformation

Think of data transformation as an adventure where you, the brave explorer, prepare your provisions for the analytical expedition ahead. Raw data often needs to be meticulously reshaped, mended, and augmented before it can reveal its hidden secrets. Let's delve deeper into this essential step.

Why Transformation is Key

- **Tailoring Data to Your Tools:** Real-world data rarely arrives in the pristine format required by your analytical weapons of choice. Transformation makes it compatible – allowing you to wield spreadsheets, databases, or advanced statistical modeling with confidence.
- **Eliminating Errors for Trustworthy Results:** Inconsistent formatting, erroneous entries, or mysterious outliers can sabotage accurate insights. The transformation stage provides a chance to meticulously examine the data, weeding out issues to ensure the integrity of your analysis.
- **Unlocking Deeper Insights:** Raw data holds potential, but it's often unwieldy. Transformation allows you to compute new variables, combine datasets for a multi-dimensional view, or standardize values for comparative analysis. It's like adding powerful lenses to your analytical telescope.

Common Transformation Tasks

Let's delve into the essential maneuvers you'll perform during this odyssey:

1. **Data Cleaning**
   - **Filling the Void:** How you tackle missing values is a strategic decision impacting outcomes. Will you

exclude incomplete records (only if feasible!), estimate replacements through techniques like mean imputation, or deploy sophisticated model-based prediction?

- ○ **Investigating Anomalies:** Outliers can be a treasure trove or a faulty reading. Careful examination is needed. Should extreme values be excluded, 'winsorized' (adjusted to a less extreme value within the distribution), or kept as-is if they represent true customer behavior?
- ○ **Eliminating Redundancies:** Especially when merging files, duplicate entries must be located and resolved. Is the duplicated data truly identical, or could slight variations hold important clues? The solution depends on the specific context.

2. **Data Formatting and Standardization**
   - ○ **Seeking Uniformity:** Aligning date formats, currency symbols, and measurement units is surprisingly satisfying, and essential for preventing miscalculations and interpretations further down the line.
   - ○ **Text Wrangling:** Converting text to lowercase, trimming whitespace, and normalizing words (e.g., stemming to find root words like 'run' from 'runs' or 'running') makes textual data more manageable for analysis.
   - ○ **Adaptable Data Types:** Ensure numbers are stored as numerics, not text, for calculations. Convert text-based dates to a computer-readable format to analyze trends over time seamlessly.

3. **Data Enrichment**
   - ○ **The Power of Computation:** Calculate new metrics that expose hidden patterns, such as customer churn probability, product performance ratios, or market share analysis over time.

- o **Weaving Data Tapestries:** Meticulously linking datasets with joins and merges builds context. Combining transaction data with customer information can reveal buying patterns unique to certain demographics or geographic areas.
- o **Expanding Horizons with External Data:** Overlaying weather trends on sales data could explain seasonality, while enriching location data with census information allows for demographic analysis on a larger scale.

4. **Data Transformation for Specific Analysis Types**
   - o **Scaling for Fair Comparison:** Normalization or standardization techniques ensure variables with drastically different ranges don't skew analyses like regression.
   - o **Categorizing the Continuous:** Binning (discretization) can transform age into age ranges, simplifying analysis and sometimes enhancing visualization clarity.
   - o **Language to Numbers:** One-hot encoding turns categorical features (like product color) into forms analyzable by machine learning models.
   - o **NLP Pre-Processing:** Tokenization (splitting text into words), stemming/lemmatization (reducing words to base forms), and removing common 'stop words' are often pre-requisites for textual analysis and topic modeling.

Tools for the Transformation Journey

- **Spreadsheets:** Ideal for light transformations, their visual nature aids in understanding the impact of your changes.
- **SQL:** Its power shines when transforming data directly within databases, especially with complex joins or aggregations.

- **Programming Languages (Python, R):** For ultimate control, these give you the reins. Mastering libraries like Pandas (Python) or dplyr (R) will significantly boost your transformation efficiency.
- **Specialized ETL Tools:** In enterprise settings with intricate data pipelines and scheduled transformations, these platforms streamline the entire workflow.

Additional Resources

- **Data Preparation Techniques for Data Mining**
  https://www.kdnuggets.com/2021/06/data-preparation-techniques-data-mining.html
- **An introduction to 'dplyr' in R for data manipulation**
  https://www.datacamp.com/community/tutorials/tutorial-on-dplyr-package-in-r
- **A Gentle Introduction to Tidy Data with R**
  (https://www.jstatsoft.org/article/view/v059i10)

Important Note: Transformation is often an iterative process. As you uncover insights, you might circle back to create new metrics, try different standardization methods, or enrich your original dataset further. Embrace the flexibility!

Ready to witness the fruits of your labor? Next, in 'Destination Insights: Arriving at Data Analysis', we'll finally unleash the power of your transformed data to answer your burning questions!

Destination Insights: Arriving at Data Analysis

After carefully collecting your data and meticulously preparing it for the journey, you now stand at the edge of discovery! This is where you harness those hard-earned datasets, choosing the right analytical methods to illuminate answers to the questions motivating your entire investigation.

Recall the Three Pillars

As a quick refresher, let's revisit the pillars of data analytics that will guide your actions:

- **Descriptive Analytics:** Summarizes past data. Tells you what *has* happened.
- **Diagnostic Analytics:** Drills down for explanations. Answers why something happened.
- **Predictive/Prescriptive Analytics:** Builds on the past to anticipate the future and suggest optimal actions.

Choosing Your Analytical Weapons

The techniques at your disposal are extensive. Let's match common analysis types to the business questions they address:

1. **Basic Statistics to Describe the Landscape**
   - **Measures of Central Tendency:** Mean, median, and mode tell you the 'typical' value in your dataset.
   - **Measures of Spread:** Standard deviation, range, and quartiles reveal how widely distributed your values are.
   - **Tabulations and Frequencies:** Summarize categorical data (e.g., how many customers fall into each 'age group' category).

2. **Questions Answered:**
   - What's the average sales volume over the last year?
   - What percentage of customers are classified as 'high spenders'?

3. **Finding Relationships with Correlation and Regression**
   - **Correlation Analysis:** Measures the *strength* and *direction* of a relationship between two numerical variables. Is there a positive or negative link between ad spending and revenue?
   - **Regression Analysis:** Builds models to *predict* a specific outcome. How much will sales *increase* for every additional dollar spent on advertising?

4. **Questions Answered:**
   - Is website dwell time related to likelihood of purchase?
   - Can we predict customer lifetime value based on early purchases?

5. **Time Series Analysis:**
   - **Unveiling Trends & Seasonality:** Specialized techniques decompose data into components, revealing if there's an overall upward trend vs. regular seasonal dips and spikes.
   - **Forecasting the Future:** Using historical patterns to predict future sales, inventory requirements, or website traffic.

6. **Questions Answered:**
   - How are product sales trending over the past several quarters?
   - What sales volume should we anticipate in the holiday season?

7. **Hypothesis Testing for Informed Decisions**
   - **Evaluating Claims:** Do two marketing campaigns have *significantly* different conversion rates, or is the difference likely due to chance?

- o **Determining Differences:** Did average customer satisfaction scores improve after process changes?

8. **Questions Answered**
   - o Is the new website design outperforming the old one?
   - o Is there a meaningful difference in defect rates between production facilities?

9. **Classification and Machine Learning (For the Complex)**
   - o **Classifying Customers:** Predict which customers are likely to churn, or respond to a new promotion, based on their characteristics.
   - o **Sentiment Analysis:** Analyze social media chatter or reviews to gauge overall opinion towards your brand or product.
   - o **Detecting Anomalies:** Identify unusual transactions for fraud detection, or unexpected spikes in machine performance data to signal potential maintenance needs.

10. **Questions Answered:**
    - o Which leads have the highest potential to convert into paying customers?
    - o Is overall customer sentiment trending positive or negative this month?
    - o Are there unusual patterns in server load that warrant investigation?

The Art of Visualization: Seeing is Understanding

Charts and graphs are your most powerful companions once analysis is underway. Choose the right ones for clarity:

- **Trends:** Line charts excel at visualizing changes over time.
- **Comparisons:** Bar charts clearly compare categories (sales by region).
- **Distribution:** Histograms show how your data is spread out.

- **Relationships:** Scatter plots reveal potential correlations between two variables.

The Importance of Context and Storytelling

Never forget, numbers don't exist in isolation! Frame insights within the business context and tie them back to the original questions that sparked your analysis:

- **"So What?" Factor:** A 5% sales increase is pointless if the goal was 15%.
- **Recommendations:** Translate findings into action – how will this knowledge change decisions?

Additional Resources

- **Choosing the Right Statistical Test** (https://stats.idre.ucla.edu/other/mult-pkg/whatstat/) (helpful guide)
- **The Power of Data Storytelling** https://www.tableau.com/learn/articles/data-storytelling

The journey doesn't end here! Data analysis is iterative – with insights leading to further questions, refined hypotheses, and a deeper understanding of the forces shaping your business. Let's now venture into 'Data Essentials', where we'll solidify key concepts and terminology.

Section 7:
Data Essentials:
Concepts and Terminology

The Data Lexicon: Essential Concepts Explored

Think of this chapter as your compass – a guide to the language of data analytics. Understanding these key terms will empower you to communicate findings, comprehend discussions, and deepen your knowledge within this exciting field.

Let's break down the fundamentals:

Data-Related

- **Data:** Raw facts, figures, observations, or measurements. It can be structured (numbers in a spreadsheet), semi-structured (like in JSON), or unstructured (free-form text).
- **Dataset:** A collection of related data, often organized into a table-like format.
- **Variable:** A characteristic being measured or observed (e.g., customer age, product price, website visit duration).
- **Observation:** A single data point representing one instance of your data (e.g., one customer's information in a row).
- **Metadata:** "Data about data." Provides context, such as variable definitions, data source, or date of collection.

Types of Data

- **Quantitative:** Numerical data. Can be discrete (counts) or continuous (measurements).
- **Qualitative:** Categorical or descriptive data. Can be nominal (unordered categories) or ordinal (categories with ranking).
- **Structured:** Easily organized into rows and columns with defined formats.
- **Unstructured:** Lacking a pre-defined structure, like free-form text, images, or audio.
- **Big Data**: Datasets too large or complex for traditional analysis, often requiring specialized tools.

Data Analysis Foundations

- **Descriptive Statistics**
    - **Mean:** The average value.
    - **Median:** The middle value in your dataset.
    - **Mode:** The most frequently occurring value.
    - **Standard Deviation:** Measures how spread out your data is around the mean.
    - **Distribution:** The overall shape of how the values in your data are spread out.
- **Correlation:** The relationship between two variables. Positive correlation means they change in the same direction; negative means opposite directions.
- **Hypothesis Testing:** A statistical framework to evaluate claims about your data with a level of certainty.
- **Statistical Significance:** A result is significant if it's unlikely to occur by chance, lending support to a hypothesis.

Analytics Techniques and Concepts

- **Regression:** Modeling the relationship between variables to make predictions.

- **Time Series Analysis:** Techniques for analyzing data over time to find trends, seasonality, or make forecasts.
- **Machine Learning:** Algorithms that learn patterns from data, used for prediction, classification, and more.
    - **Supervised Learning:** Using labeled data to train models for a specific task (e.g., classifying email as spam/not spam).
    - **Unsupervised Learning:** Identifying patterns in unlabeled data (e.g., clustering customers into groups).
- **Data Visualization:** Representing data graphically (bar charts, scatter plots, etc.) to reveal patterns and communicate insights.

Data in Action: The Business Context

- **KPI (Key Performance Indicator):** A measurable metric that tracks progress towards business goals.
- **Dashboard:** A visual display of multiple KPIs in a single place, monitoring real-time performance.
- **A/B Testing:** Comparing two versions (e.g., website designs) to identify which performs better.
- **ROI (Return on Investment):** A measure of profitability, evaluating the efficiency of investments or actions.
- **Churn Rate:** The percentage of customers that stop doing business with a company in a specific timeframe.

Data Governance and Ethics

- **Data Privacy:** The responsible handling of personal data in compliance with laws like the GDPR and CCPA.
- **Data Security:** Protecting data from breaches, unauthorized access, or alteration.
- **Data Bias:** Unintentional skewing of data caused by how it's collected or used. This can lead to misleading or unfair model outcomes.

Additional Resources

- **Glossary of Statistical Terms**
  https://www.statsref.com/HTML/glossary.html
- **Khan Academy: Statistics and Probability**
  (https://www.khanacademy.org/math/statistics-probability)

Key Takeaway: This vocabulary serves as your foundation. As you delve deeper into data analysis, you'll discover even more specialized terms Continuously expanding your data lexicon is a hallmark of growth in the field!

Ready for a fun reinforcement of these terms? Let's move onto 'Flashcards of Knowledge: Key Terminology Unveiled' for a quick and interactive review!

Flashcards of Knowledge: Key Terminology Unveiled

It's time to test and solidify your understanding of essential data analytics terminology. This chapter provides virtual flashcards for quick and engaging review. Consider cutting these out as physical flashcards or using online flashcard apps for on-the-go learning!

Instructions

1. Read the term on the "front" of each flashcard.
2. Try to recall its definition or explanation.
3. Flip to the "back" of the card to check your understanding, and reread the explanation if needed.
4. Repeat for all flashcards, shuffling for variety.

FRONT: Data **BACK:** Raw facts, figures, observations, or measurements. Data comes in many forms, including structured (spreadsheets), semi-structured (JSON), and unstructured (text, images).

FRONT: Variable **BACK:** A characteristic or attribute that you measure or collect in your data. Examples: customer age, website visit duration, product type.

FRONT: Descriptive Statistics **BACK:** Methods for summarizing and describing the key characteristics of a dataset. Examples include mean, median, standard deviation, and visualizations.

FRONT: Correlation **BACK:** A statistical measure that indicates the extent to which two variables are linearly related (positive, negative, or no correlation).

FRONT: Hypothesis Testing **BACK:** A framework for evaluating whether the results you observed in your data are likely due to real effects or simply random chance.

FRONT: Regression **BACK:** A technique for modeling the relationship between variables to make predictions. For example, predicting sales based on advertising spend.

FRONT: Machine Learning (ML) **BACK:** A field where algorithms "learn" patterns from data without explicit programming. ML powers tasks like image classification, customer churn prediction, and recommendation systems.

FRONT: KPI (Key Performance Indicator) **BACK:** A quantifiable metric that businesses track to measure progress towards critical goals. Examples include revenue, website traffic, and customer satisfaction.

FRONT: Data Visualization **BACK:** The graphical representation of data to uncover insights and communicate findings. Think of charts like bar charts, line graphs, scatter plots, and more.

FRONT: A/B Testing **BACK:** A method to compare two or more versions of something (like website designs) to identify the highest performing option.

FRONT: Big Data **BACK:** Extremely large and complex datasets that exceed the capabilities of traditional analysis tools. Big Data often exhibits the "4 V's" - Volume, Velocity, Variety, Veracity.

FRONT: Data Privacy **BACK:** Responsible and ethical handling of personal information, adhering to regulations like GDPR (Europe) and CCPA (California).

FRONT: Data Bias **BACK:** Systematic errors in how data is collected or used, leading to models that perpetuate unfairness or discrimination. Being aware of bias is crucial for responsible analytics.

Expand Your Flashcard Deck

As you continue your data journey, add new terms you encounter to your growing collection of flashcards!

Additional Resources

- **Quizlet** https://quizlet.com/ – Create your own digital flashcards
- **Anki** (https://apps.ankiweb.net/) - Popular flashcard app with spaced repetition for efficient learning

Congratulations! You're actively building a solid foundation in the language of data. Let's continue by exploring exciting learning paths for your data journey in 'Charting Your Course: Navigating the Data Learning Landscape'.

Section 8:
Crafting Your Data Journey: Learning and Career Paths

Charting Your Course: Navigating the Data Learning Landscape

The field of data analytics is always evolving. Embracing lifelong learning is essential in order to stay ahead of the curve. Let's explore the diverse paths to knowledge, helping you map out a personalized journey to match your ambitions.

Step 1: Assess Your Starting Point

- **Beginner:** If you're entirely new to data analysis, focus on building a foundation. Start with the core concepts, data types, and simple statistics.
- **Some Experience:** Perhaps you've used spreadsheets extensively but want to delve deeper. Identify your strengths and the specific skills you wish to acquire.
- **Career Changer:** You might have strong domain knowledge in another field. In that case, focus on data skills specifically relevant to your industry and desired role.

Step 2: Explore Learning Formats

There's something for everyone! Consider which fits your learning style best:

- **Structured Courses:**
  - o **Online platforms:** Coursera, Udemy, DataCamp, edX offer both free and paid courses, often with certificates upon completion.
  - o **University Programs:** Ideal for in-depth study and a formal credential. Look for degrees/certificates in Data Science, Business Analytics. Some universities offer online options as well.
- **Books & Textbooks:** Perfect if you enjoy self-paced, in-depth learning. (Perhaps even one like the book you're writing!)
- **Interactive Tutorials:** Websites like Codecademy provide hands-on practice as you code along, ideal for learning programming skills.
- **Blogs & Articles:** Keep up with current trends and best practices by following reputable data blogs and online publications.
- **Documentation:** Never underestimate the power of official documentation for the specific tools you want to master!

Step 3: Focus Areas to Deepen Your Expertise

- **Data Fundamentals:** Databases with SQL, statistics, understanding data collection and biases. A solid foundation is essential.
- **Programming:** Python and R are the powerhouses of data analysis. Choose one to start, and you can branch out later as needed.
- **Data Visualization:** Tools like Tableau, Power BI, or even coding libraries (ggplot2 in R, Matplotlib in Python) to create compelling visualizations.

- **Big Data Technologies:** If you anticipate working with massive datasets, explore tools like Hadoop, Spark, and cloud-based solutions.
- **Machine Learning:** Delve into algorithms (from basic regression to advanced neural networks) for prediction, classification, and understanding complex data relationships.
- **Domain Specialization:** Tailor your learning to your career goals. Pick up industry-specific skills: healthcare analytics, financial modeling, marketing analytics, etc.

Step 4: Learning Beyond Courses

- **Projects Are Key:** Apply your skills! Find public datasets (Kaggle, government portals) or tackle a problem that interests you. The true learning happens by doing.
- **Community Connection:** Join online forums, attend meetups (virtual or in-person) to network. Ask questions, learn from others, and even collaborate on projects.
- **Showcase Your Work:** Build a portfolio on GitHub or a personal website to demonstrate your skills to potential employers.
- **Teach to Truly Learn:** Blogging, creating tutorials, or answering questions on forums will solidify your own understanding.

Additional Resources

- **Open Source Data Science Masters**
  https://github.com/datasciencemasters/go

Staying Motivated on Your Journey

- **Set Small Goals:** Break big goals into achievable steps for continuous progress.
- **Find Your Tribe:** Engage with online communities of fellow learners.

- **Celebrate Wins:** Acknowledge your milestones, no matter how small!
- **Never Stop Being Curious:** The data world is dynamic – stay updated with newsletters and podcasts tailored to your interests

The path to mastery is a continuous one. Our final chapter, 'Career Paths in Data Analytics: Mapping Your Professional Journey' will explore the vast range of roles you could pursue in this exciting field!

Career Paths in Data Analytics: Mapping Your Professional Journey

The field of data analytics is booming, with businesses across all industries recognizing the immense value it unlocks. This translates to a multitude of diverse career opportunities. Let's explore popular routes, keeping in mind new specializations are always emerging!

Core Data Analyst Roles

- **Data Analyst:** The backbone role! You'll clean, transform, analyze, and visualize data to answer business questions, extract trends, and support decision-making.
- **Business Analyst:** Blends data with business domain knowledge. Focuses on identifying process improvements, translating data into actionable recommendations for stakeholders.
- **Database Administrator (DBA):** Ensures databases run smoothly. Designs, implements, maintains, and optimizes access/security for the entire organization's data storage.
- **Data Engineer:** Builds the pipelines! Designs and maintains the infrastructure to collect, store, and process large-scale data for analysis by others.

Specialized Paths

- **Data Scientist:** Often requires advanced degrees. Applies machine learning, strong statistics, and sometimes coding to build models for prediction, classification, and clustering tasks.

- **Marketing Analyst:** Dives into customer data, campaign performance, social media metrics, etc., to optimize marketing strategies and ROI.
- **Financial Analyst:** Leverages data to assess financial health, forecast future performance, and guide investment strategies.
- **Healthcare Data Analyst:** Analyzes patient data, clinical trial outcomes, healthcare costs, and operational efficiency. Their insights are crucial for driving improvements in care delivery.
- **Risk Analyst:** Uses data-driven models to assess and predict potential risks in fields like finance, insurance, and security, managing exposure and preventative measures.
- **BI Developer:** Masters data visualization tools (Tableau, Power BI) to create interactive, real-time dashboards and reports, empowering non-technical users to gain insights.

Factors Influencing Your Career Path

- **Industry:** Each sector has unique data and challenges, opening doors to specialized roles.
- **Company Size:** Startups call for generalists who wear multiple hats; corporations can have highly specialized positions.
- **Skill Depth:** Choose a narrow focus with deep expertise (e.g., NLP expert), or be a generalist with broad skills across the entire data pipeline.
- **Desired Level of "Coding":** Roles can range from less coding-intensive (using visual tools) to heavily focused on programming and algorithm development.

Preparing to Embark on Your Data Career

1. **Build the Skillset:** Previous chapters guide your learning journey. Focus on the core skills AND those specifically relevant to your desired domain.

2. **Portfolio Speaks Louder:** Your projects are your resume! Demonstrate your skills through public datasets or real-world problem-solving examples.
3. **Network Strategically:** Attend industry events, connect with people in your desired roles. Mentorship can be invaluable.
4. **Tailor Your Resume:** Keyword-match your resume and cover letter to the specific job requirements of each role you apply for.
5. **The Power of Storytelling:** Practice communicating your analysis in ways that resonate with business stakeholders – turn data into compelling narratives.

Additional Resources

- **Data Science Central** https://www.datasciencecentral.com/: Great job boards & community
- **Analytics Vidhya** (https://www.analyticsvidhya.com/) : Extensive resource for both learning and career content
- **Towards Data Science** (https://towardsdatascience.com/): Popular blog with diverse articles

The Evolving Future of Data Careers

New specializations and titles are bound to emerge as data technology advances. Focus on:

- **Responsible AI:** Ensuring fairness and transparency in data-driven models becomes more critical than ever.
- **Data Storyteller:** As organizations become data-savvy, the skill of turning complex analysis into compelling narratives is increasingly valuable.

The world of data analytics is your oyster! Your interests, skills, and consistent effort will guide your unique and fulfilling career path. This concludes our handbook, but your

data journey is just beginning. Best of luck as you embark on this exciting adventure!

Conclusion

Throughout this handbook, we've embarked on an exciting expedition. You've ventured into the depths of data, grasped its diverse forms, navigated a vast ecosystem of tools, and discovered the power of transforming raw information into actionable insights.

Key Reminders from Your Journey

- **Data is Everywhere:** From spreadsheets to social media chatter, every industry relies on data. The modern world runs on it.
- **Tools Are Empowering:** Whether embracing code or user-friendly interfaces, tools enhance your ability to manipulate and unlock the stories within your data.
- **Analysis is Iterative:** Rarely is it a straight path from question to answer. The best analysts are curious, experiment, and refine their approaches.
- **Communication is Key:** Data needs a voice. The most brilliant findings are useless unless compellingly conveyed to influence real-world decisions.
- **Ethics Matter:** Remember the weight of responsibility – handle data ethically, be aware of biases, and champion transparency.

The Adventure Continues...

This handbook served as your compass and provisions, equipping you with the foundational knowledge for success. Yet, the landscape of data analytics is always changing. Embrace these principles for continued growth:

- **Be a Lifelong Learner:** Dedicate yourself to continuous learning. New technologies and methodologies will emerge – staying up-to-date is critical.
- **The Community is Your Ally:** Connect with fellow data enthusiasts! This is a supportive field where sharing knowledge and collaborating leads to collective breakthroughs.
- **Apply Your Skills:** Seek opportunities, big or small, to tackle real-world problems. Every project hones your skillset and builds your confidence.

The Power of Data-Driven Decision Making

In a world overflowing with data, those who harness it effectively hold an incredible advantage. Businesses make smarter strategic moves. Scientists push the boundaries of discovery. Individuals gain a deeper understanding of their own behavior and patterns.

Your data analytics journey gives you the ability to impact the world in meaningful ways. Whether you aspire to lead data teams, revolutionize your industry, or simply become a more informed consumer of information, the skills you've gained are invaluable.

Go Forth and Decode!

May your curiosity never cease and your passion for uncovering hidden truths propel you forward. The world of data awaits your insightful analysis!